LEGACY-LINES EXPLORER

EMMA HAYES

*Her Legacy, family, Triumphs, and her Transformative
Journey Through Coaching*

Disclaimer

The information presented in this book is intended solely for educational and informational purposes. Every effort has been made to ensure the accuracy of the insights, trends, and analyses included herein. However, due to the rapidly changing nature of markets, consumer behaviors, and evolving trends, some information may become outdated or open to interpretation. Readers are encouraged to verify details and consult current sources for the most up-to-date information. The author and publisher disclaim any liability for decisions made based on the content of this book.

First edition

This book was professionally typeset on Reedsy.
Find out more at reedsy.com

Contents

Introduction

Emma Hayes is more than simply a talented coach; she is a revolutionary leader whose impact has changed the face of women's soccer throughout the world. Hayes' path, from her early days at Chelsea FC to her revolutionary position with the United States Women's National Team (USWNT), exemplifies a pioneering mentality propelled by tenacity, ingenuity, and an uncompromising devotion to greatness. Hayes, known for her tactical acumen and ability to build supportive, winning situations, has not only won incredible triumphs but also inspired a new generation of athletes to push the limits of what is possible in athletics.

Hayes' career is a lesson in blending strategy with sensitivity. Her teams play with freedom and excitement, which has resulted in record-breaking success, including several Women's Super League (WSL) crowns with Chelsea and a gold medal in the 2024 Olympics with the USWNT. Each stage of her journey demonstrates her commitment to her teammates' growth both on and off the field, showing her comprehensive approach to leadership.

This book will look at significant themes in Hayes' life, including perseverance in the face of adversity, innovation in a traditional sport, and the force of inclusiveness. Readers will learn about her unwavering pursuit of equality, her distinct coaching style, which stresses honesty and emotional intelligence, and her lasting impact as a pioneer in women's soccer. As readers start on this trip, they will discover that Hayes' success stems not just from her technical acumen but also from her profound grasp of the human aspect of sport—a lesson that applies well beyond the field and into every sector where genuine leadership is required.

Chapter 1

Early Life and Family Background

Emma Hayes was born on October 18, 1976, in Camden, London, into a world full of variety, energy, and challenge. Camden, noted for its diverse cultural mix, was a setting that valued resilience, which would become one of Hayes' hallmarks. Her area was filled with the sounds and sights of London's working-class neighborhoods, where football was more than just a sport—it was a way of life, an escape, and a source of hope for many.

Hayes' family was influential in shaping her personality, emphasizing ideals such as hard work, loyalty, and bravery. Though little is known publicly about her parents, it is clear from her interviews and accomplishments that they were strongly supportive of her, even when her desires led her down a less-traveled path for young females at the time. Her parents' continuous support for her athletic endeavors, despite societal standards, let her recognize the potential of an alternative path—one in which gender did not limit ambition.

Growing up, Emma was a naturally competitive youngster who was constantly looking for new challenges. Her parents often encouraged her to explore hobbies that enabled her to channel her energy, particularly athletics, and they never stopped her from following her own interests. Her mother, in particular, was a tremendous inspiration, demonstrating the perseverance and independence that Emma would later emulate in her profession. She often remembers her mother emphasizing compassion, honesty, and the need to stand up for oneself—characteristics that formed the core of Hayes' teaching approach and entire view on life.

Camden's distinctive cultural tapestry exposed Emma to a diverse range of cultures, languages, and viewpoints from a young age. Her neighborhood was united by football, and she quickly absorbed the local passion for the sport. In the surrounding streets, she saw boys play with unbridled enthusiasm, frequently joining in despite her young age and little size. While many girls her age might have pursued other hobbies, Emma found her tribe among the guys on the field, where her talent and tenacity rapidly gained her respect.

This setting taught her the value of inclusion and adaptation, which she would use throughout her career as she strived to bring out the best in every team she coached, regardless of background or assumptions. Camden was also a location where Hayes had to learn to establish himself—qualities that would later prove important in his path through the male-dominated world of soccer. She was never one to back down, and she rapidly learned how to manage herself with larger and older males, building mental fortitude that would serve her well later in life.

Emma's passion for football began at a young age, and she was continuously watching any local game. Since there were few and underfunded girls' soccer leagues, Emma quickly joined the local male teams. Her ability and agility struck out right away, enabling her to gain a spot even among the older players. Although joining boys' teams was unusual and difficult, the experiences sharpened her ambition and fearlessness, traits that would later become important to her career.

Acceptance into the Arsenal Academy was a watershed moment in her young life. Despite the underrepresentation of female players at the time, Emma's perseverance earned her a slot. The program provided her with an essential insight into the competitive world of professional soccer, pushing her to pursue her ambition of playing at the top level. She engaged herself in training, driven by a desire to succeed, and swiftly established herself as a prospective talent inside the institution. However, a major ankle injury at the age of 17 abruptly cut short her goal.

The injury was catastrophic, forcing her to forsake her dreams of a professional playing career. For any young athlete, such an accident is a devastating setback, and for Hayes, it meant facing the realities of a new direction. Rather than allowing her disappointment to define her, she looked for ways to be involved in the sport she loved, focusing her efforts on teaching. This experience of loss and redirection taught her a lesson that she would later share with her players: losses, although painful, may lead to unexpected and sometimes transformational new chances.

Following the injury, Emma attended university in Liverpool, where she continued to pursue her passion for soccer by coaching the women's team. Her transition into coaching was not intentional but rather a natural evolution as she developed a love for teaching and encouraging others. This early journey into coaching provided her with a sense of purpose, enabling her to share her love of soccer with others while also developing her own leadership style.

These early coaching experiences highlighted her talent for seeing potential in players that others may ignore. Her personal experiences as an outsider on boys' teams enabled her to sympathize with athletes who faced difficulties. As she subsequently said, these formative years taught her the virtues of patience, perseverance, and the need to create a friendly environment—philosophies she brought with her to every team she led.

Hayes grew up with ideals that included empathy, bravery, and respect for uniqueness. Her Camden background, with its ethnic diversity and socioeconomic intricacies, provided her a unique perspective on the value of teamwork and inclusion. These concepts would frame her coaching philosophy, which emphasized player development as a whole rather than simply athletic achievement. She viewed soccer as a platform for not just technical development but also character development—a viewpoint that would set her apart as a coach.

Emma realized throughout her coaching career that success in soccer required more than simply technical ability. She stressed mental resilience, emotional intelligence, and the capacity to function as a cohesive unit from the beginning of her leadership career. She instilled in her players the value of individual and group responsibility, urging them to see the game as a metaphor for life's larger difficulties and possibilities.

Chapter 2

Educational Foundations and Influences

Emma Hayes' school journey displays her dedication to both academic success and her love of soccer. Raised in London, Hayes attended local schools where she excelled academically and participated in athletics. She was determined to thrive academically from a young age, even while she pursued her passion for soccer. Camden's close-knit and ethnically diverse town exposed her to a variety of experiences and opinions, broadening her knowledge of people and leadership. Her work as a coach, characterized by her sensitivity and commitment to each player's unique growth, would eventually reflect these observations.

Hayes' official education began in elementary and secondary schools in her London area, where her professors recognized her innate talent for athletics and leadership. Her academic interests were diverse, and she displayed a strong curiosity, particularly in disciplines that enabled her to investigate social dynamics and team structures. Soccer, on the other hand, was her actual love, and she found methods to balance her education with her participation in local minor leagues, even joining males' teams when there were no chances for girls. This early dedication to tearing down boundaries in athletics anticipated the perseverance that would define her career.

Hayes continued her study at Liverpool Hope University after finishing high school. She earned a degree in European Studies, which enabled her to continue her interest in cultural and social institutions. Her participation in the university's soccer program supplemented her studies, providing her with her first official coaching experience with the women's squad. Hayes coupled her academic aspirations with her love of soccer at Liverpool when she discovered her coaching talent—a passion that would ultimately define her life. In interviews, she regularly noted how this era helped her comprehend the complexities of team dynamics and human connections, which she would use extensively as a coach.

During her stay in Liverpool, Hayes met various mentors who influenced her career path. One of her most impactful mentors was a coach who pushed her to consider coaching as a legitimate professional choice. His faith in her coaching abilities inspired her to envision a lasting impact in soccer, despite an injury ending her playing career. This mentoring gave her vital insights into coaching philosophy, and it was during these years that she started to build her unique leadership style, which stressed empathy, strategic thinking, and player-centered development.

Hayes' experiences in Liverpool shaped not just her teaching skills but also her personal development. The varied student population and the city's rich cultural past enlarged her viewpoint, instilling a value in inclusion and adaptation that would become key to her coaching philosophy. Her education in European education also helped her have a better knowledge of cross-cultural communication, which she used later in her work when she moved into international coaching. Furthermore, juggling scholastic expectations with coaching obligations taught her tenacity, discipline, and the value of adaptation, all of which would serve her well as she advanced in her coaching career.

Following graduation, Hayes expanded her practical experience by searching out hands-on coaching jobs in London and subsequently the United States. She took on her first important coaching post with the Long Island Lady Riders, a United Soccer League club based in the United States. This transition forced her to swiftly adjust to new cultural and tactical demands, which she welcomed with gusto. Her stay in the United States exposed her to other coaching theories and approaches, which helped her develop her own approach. Here, she also met some significant personalities in

American soccer who provided her advice and encouragement. Working with experienced coaches broadened Hayes' grasp of player psychology, training methodologies, and match preparations.

While coaching in the United States, Hayes pursued more studies to improve her abilities. She sought coaching certifications and credentials, which required extensive training and supervision from recognized leaders in the sport. These credentials not only boosted her technical knowledge but also increased her feeling of legitimacy in the competitive world of soccer coaching. Her dedication to lifelong learning distinguished her as a coach eager to change and adapt, characteristics that would characterize her career.

Notable coaching personalities, particularly Arsène Wenger, the former manager of Arsenal FC, inspired Hayes as she gained experience. She appreciated Wenger's focus on player development and his ability to strike a balance between tactical discipline and creative flexibility, which she would later integrate into her own coaching style. Hayes' holistic approach to coaching, emphasizing not only athletic success but also her players' personal development and well-being, reflects Wenger's influence. She has often cited Wenger's emphasis on developing players as persons as a paradigm that resonated strongly with her and informed her long-term strategy.

Formal academic study, hands-on coaching experience, and mentorship from others who recognized her potential distinguished Emma Hayes's educational trajectory. Hayes' education, from her early years in Camden to her time at Liverpool Hope University and eventually her training in the United States, developed her into a smart, strategic, and sympathetic leader. Her academic background in European Studies aided her knowledge of team dynamics and cross-cultural communication, while her hands-on experience and significant mentors provided her with the skills and confidence required to flourish in soccer's competitive coaching landscape.

Hayes' educational journey was ultimately a dynamic process of self-discovery and professional development rather than a straight one. Her identity as a leader grew with each stage of her education, from early childhood to university and subsequent coaching training. Her experiences highlight the value of perseverance, adaptation, and the quest for knowledge—

qualities that have enabled her to redefine success in women's soccer and serve as a role model for aspiring coaches all around the globe. Readers may learn from her narrative that genuine leadership is based not just on technical talent but also on a dedication to personal development, empathy, and the bravery to continuously follow one's goal.

Chapter 3

Personal Life

Emma Hayes, well-known for her successes in women's soccer, has developed a secluded yet meaningful personal life that has a significant impact on her public triumphs. While she keeps a low profile about her family and relationships, she has said that her spouse is a supporting influence in her life. They prioritize mutual respect, creating shared objectives, and striking a beneficial balance between her busy profession and family responsibilities. Hayes often attributes her spouse with being her "biggest cheerleader," a source of support that enables her to concentrate on high-stakes professional tasks without jeopardizing her personal life.

Hayes is also a dedicated mother of two children, a responsibility she values much. Although she avoids discussing intimate information about her family, she publicly considers meaningful family time as critical to her well-being. Her parenting style is consistent with her coaching philosophy, with an emphasis on empowering and fostering her children's unique abilities. She has deliberately sought to strike a balance between her demanding profession and her obligations as a mother, realizing that family stability boosts her success as a field leader.

Beyond family, Hayes cultivates significant ties in the soccer world, where her kindness and devotion make her a valuable mentor to both players and coworkers. Known for her real approachability, she engages with players on a human level, creating an atmosphere in which they feel supported and understood. These intimate relationships extend to her friends and mentors, who help to strengthen her professional and personal lives by providing advice, companionship, and, on occasion, a sounding board for her ideas and plans.

In her own time, Hayes pursues a variety of activities that add to her well-rounded outlook. Reading is one of her favorite pleasures, and she often recommends encouraging books to her teammates. Cooking is another peaceful pastime she enjoys, since it allows her to chill and explore away from the stresses of coaching. She also prioritizes maintaining her physical health by regularly participating in sports such as jogging and yoga, which she views as essential for managing the demanding demands of her job.

Hayes' basic beliefs are at the heart of both her personal and professional life: empathy, inclusion, and resilience. She is deeply committed to sports equality and has advocated for women's soccer rights and possibilities. Her support for these topics extends beyond the field, as she often promotes gender equality, inspiring both present and future generations of female athletes. Her ideals influence her public image as a coach who not only leads winning teams but also works to foster a healthy and supportive sports culture.

Overall, Emma Hayes' personal connections, principles, and interests serve as the foundation for her professional life, allowing her to flourish publicly while remaining grounded personally. This combination of personal contentment and professional achievement makes her tale an encouraging example of reaching greatness while emphasizing meaningful relationships and ideals.

Chapter 4

Foundations of Career and Initial Successes

Emma Hayes' professional path is a compelling narrative of determination, ambition, and a desire to make a difference in women's soccer. Her journey started with rather modest coaching positions, each of which pushed her closer to the high-profile profession she would eventually have. Hayes' early employment was essential in shaping her coaching philosophy and cementing her vision for advancing women's soccer on a global scale. Her path, however, was fraught with difficulties, significant persons who affected her direction, and watershed events that catapulted her from beginner coach to acknowledged professional.

Emma Hayes' soccer career did not begin with aspirations to teach; she first wanted to be a player. After a catastrophic ankle injury terminated her professional playing dreams at the age of 17, she focused on teaching while attending Liverpool Hope University. Hayes took on her first coaching job with the university's women's team, where she learned about the complexities of team leadership and demonstrated her natural ability to guide others.

Hayes moved to the United States after finishing her degree, marking her first important step into professional coaching. Her early career in America started with the Long Island Lady Riders of the W-League, an atmosphere that was both difficult and inspirational. The W-competition was a semi-professional competition that taught Hayes about team administration in a setting with limited resources and big objectives. These early years taught her tenacity, flexibility, and the capacity to develop new solutions—all of which she would use throughout her career.

Rapid recognition of Hayes' coaching abilities led to her appointment as the head coach of the women's soccer team at Iona College in New Rochelle, New York. Hayes started to hone her coaching philosophy, emphasizing player development and creating a friendly team atmosphere. She had to establish a competitive team at Iona with minimal resources, a task that tested her ingenuity and leadership skills. She established a disciplined training routine that stressed both talent and collaboration, setting a high bar for her players. This was Hayes' first experience in college coaching, and she learned how to combine physical achievement with her players' academic and personal requirements.

Her years at Iona were pivotal, as she found that coaching was more than just tactics; it was also about knowing and developing individual players. This approach became crucial to her career and separated her from other coaches, establishing her as a thoughtful and player-focused leader. Hayes gained important experience at Iona before returning to England to become an assistant coach for Arsenal's women's squad. This role exposed her to a higher level of play and allowed her to learn from Arsenal's successful system while working with key people in women's soccer. Her time at Arsenal taught her the value of intense training, tactical preparation, and overall player development. As a member of a famous club, Hayes saw firsthand what an elite coaching infrastructure looked like, motivating her desire to set comparable standards in her future positions.

Hayes returned to the United States in 2008, taking over as head coach of the Chicago Red Stars in the newly founded Women's Professional Soccer (WPS) league. The Red Stars were her first significant chance to oversee a club in a totally professional context. Hayes had the arduous job of assembling a competitive roster in a league that was still establishing its feet. The WPS had various hurdles, including restricted media coverage, budgetary limits, and battling for recognition in a male-dominated sports industry. Despite these challenges, Hayes led with her customary zeal and tactical acumen, attempting to develop a unified team identity while instilling resilience in her teammates.

The WPS experience was beneficial because it prompted Hayes to devise new methods to manage her club in the face of periodic financial insecurity and the league's quest for viability. During this period, Hayes developed ties with other players and staff members who valued her passion and progressive approach. Although the league finally failed, the experience taught her vital lessons about persistence and flexibility, cementing her image as a fervent supporter of women's soccer.

After her stint with the Red Stars, Hayes returned to England when Chelsea FC Women named her head coach in 2012. This role was a watershed event in her career since it gave her the opportunity to execute her ideas on a broader scale. Hayes joined Chelsea at a period when women's soccer in England was gaining traction, but resources were still short and teams were striving to establish themselves as competitive and long-term institutions.

Hayes embraced her work at Chelsea with the intention of creating not just a great squad but also a lasting institution in women's soccer. She pushed for more cash, better training facilities, and a more professional atmosphere for her players. Her aim went beyond the pitch; she wanted to elevate the prominence of women's soccer and create a more egalitarian system for female players. Under her guidance, Chelsea developed from a tiny club into a powerhouse of women's soccer, winning many Women's Super League (WSL) championships and constantly competing at the highest level. Hayes received encouragement and assistance from important soccer mentors during her career. Arsène Wenger, the former Arsenal manager, was one of her early inspirations, and his approach to player development and strategic vision spoke to her strongly. Wenger's idea of empowering players and cultivating a unified team culture influenced Hayes' techniques, which stress player autonomy and adaptation. Similarly, Hayes' experiences with her Arsenal teammates served as an example of professionalism and tactical skill, which she would bring to Chelsea.

Hayes built outstanding connections with her Chelsea players, winning their trust and respect by investing in their personal development. She encouraged them to pursue their own ambitions, fostering a supportive atmosphere in which players felt respected. Her dedication to her players' growth and well-being made her a standout figure in coaching, and many athletes who worked with her characterized her as both a coach and a mentor.

Hayes had various hurdles as she sought to transform Chelsea into a premier squad. In her early years, finances were scarce, and women's soccer battled to gain prominence. She campaigned for equal access to facilities, better contracts, and a more professional environment, meeting opposition but persevering in her attempts to enhance the women's team's reputation inside the club. These efforts paid off, as Chelsea started to recruit elite players and achieve success in both local and European tournaments.

Numerous historic milestones, including leading the club to several league victories and becoming the first female manager to reach a UEFA Women's Champions League final in more than a decade, have highlighted her time at Chelsea. Her achievement has not only lifted Chelsea but also established a new standard for women's soccer in England and around Europe.

Emma Hayes' early career demonstrates her perseverance, versatility, and steadfast devotion to promoting women's soccer. Hayes has continually pushed limits, converting every squad she has managed into a more competitive and cohesive organization. Her rise from inexperienced coach to one of the most revered people in women's soccer exemplifies the strength of perseverance, visionary leadership, and the significance of promoting equality in sports.

Chapter 5

Key Achievements, Recognition, and Legacy Contributions

From her time with Chelsea FC Women to her current role as head coach of the United States Women's National Team, Emma Hayes' career has been characterized by unprecedented successes. Her professional experience demonstrates her ability to construct successful teams, her unique coaching techniques, and her commitment to growing women's soccer internationally.

Hayes swiftly set her eyes on changing Chelsea from a modest competitor to a European soccer powerhouse after joining the club in 2012. During her time, Chelsea Women won six Women's Super League (WSL) crowns, five FA Cups, and two League Cups. Hayes' strategic philosophy, emphasizing both strong defensive organization and explosive attacking play, revolutionized women's soccer in England. Chelsea achieved an unprecedented feat by reaching the 2021 UEFA Women's Champions League final, but Barcelona ultimately defeated them. This near-victory demonstrates Hayes' effectiveness in elevating Chelsea's prominence to a level previously unmatched by English women's teams.

Her accomplishments at Chelsea earned her countless personal honors. FIFA voted Hayes the FIFA Women's Coach of the Year in 2021, recognizing her leadership and consistent success in both local and European tournaments. This award confirmed her place as one of the sport's top managers, emphasizing her role in raising the quality and awareness of women's soccer. In appreciation of her contributions to women's sports, she received an OBE (Officer of the Order of the British Empire), recognizing her commitment to both the game and gender equality in sports.

Hayes took over as head coach of the USWNT in 2024, guiding the team to an Olympic gold medal in Paris, the team's fifth and first since 2012. This triumph was a high point in her career, as she remarked that it was "bigger than anything else I've ever done." Her performance with the USWNT earned her instant recognition, including the first Women's Coach of the Year award from the Ballon d'Or, which recognized her effect on both Chelsea and the USWNT. This post also represented her return to the United States, where her coaching career started, and established her as a worldwide spokesperson for women's soccer.

Hayes' impact extends beyond her tactical exploits. Her work for women's rights, equitable pay, and professional development in women's soccer has had a huge impact on the business. At Chelsea, she campaigned to guarantee that her team had the same access to facilities, support personnel, and media coverage as the men's teams. This lobbying contributed to improvements not just at Chelsea but across the WSL, as other clubs started to follow Chelsea's lead in treating women's teams with similar regard. Her departure from Chelsea leaves behind a league that is more competitive and recognized on the world stage.

Chapter 6

Philosophy and Core Vision

Emma Hayes' career has been characterized by a set of fundamental beliefs that prioritize responsibility, player autonomy, and a focus on pleasure and mental resilience. Her conviction in these values has formed her coaching philosophy, influencing every squad she has managed and leaving an indelible impression on the world of women's soccer.

Hayes' coaching strategy is based on instilling a "no excuse" attitude among her squad. Hayes thinks that players and coaching staff should always hold themselves responsible for their performance, always asking, "What could we have done better?" rather than blaming individuals or outside causes. Hayes reflected on her time at Chelsea, saying, "We've created a no-excuse culture." After every game, we must look in the mirror and ask ourselves, 'What might we have done better?' "We must accept responsibility for that." She has fostered a culture that demands continuous self-improvement and eliminates any excuses. A no-excuses philosophy drove Chelsea FC Women's development into one of Europe's most competitive teams. Hayes' concept required that players critically evaluate their own conduct, whether in win or failure, fostering development and responsibility at all levels of the club. This method has earned Hayes not just a reputation as a great coach but also as a mentor who instills lifelong values in her athletes. "I think as a leader, you have to know the responsibility of your position," she pointed out. "If you allow excuses to exist, you are promoting mediocrity. I will not tolerate such behavior, as it hinders the development of others.

Hayes' coaching philosophy also emphasizes enabling players to make their own choices while fostering creativity and individual expression on the field. At Chelsea, she gave players the flexibility to experiment within a disciplined system, cultivating outstanding levels of discipline and adaptability. Hayes continued to implement this philosophy when she joined the United States Women's National Team (USWNT), allowing players to express themselves and play to their full potential. This attitude was critical to the USWNT's success in the 2024 Olympics, as the players' confidence and unity propelled them to victory.

Players have applauded Hayes' emphasis on player empowerment. Sophia Smith, a USWNT attacker, said Hayes helped the squad "rediscover who we already knew we were, but we just needed a little bit of guidance." This freedom and trust enabled the players to perform with more confidence and togetherness. Defender Naomi Girma said that Hayes "came in and allowed us to be ourselves," allowing the team to gel more successfully and achieve success.

Hayes' attitude toward empowerment extends beyond methods. She views each player as a person with distinct abilities and potential, and her coaching style is very player-centered. Hayes makes athletes feel loved and understood by fostering a supportive atmosphere, which contributes to a trust-based high-performance culture. Her emphasis on individual development has made her a recognized figure off the field, as players believe her mentoring and counsel extend beyond soccer.

Hayes realizes that athletic achievement is more than simply physical; it is also profoundly emotional and mental. Hayes has placed a strong emphasis on fun, friendship, and mental health during her tenure at both Chelsea and the USWNT. Music, laughter, and a sense of fun characterize her training sessions, which not only reduce stress but also foster player relationships. This positive environment significantly contributed to the USWNT's victory in 2024, as the team's cohesiveness and confidence were evident throughout the tournament. Trinity Rodman, one of the team's star players, said, "The fun aspect goes a little bit unseen in sports, but I think it was huge for us."

She emphasized how Hayes' fostering of pleasure resulted in greater ties on and off the field.

Hayes' focus on mental resilience stems from his knowledge of the psychological demands that athletes undergo. She cultivates a culture that encourages players to relish the game while maintaining a calm demeanor in the face of pressure. Hayes explained: "It's not just about the tactics; it's about giving players the tools to navigate life's challenges with confidence." Her emphasis on perseverance has resonated with her players, who view her as a mentor in both sports and life, and appreciate her comprehensive approach to teaching.

Hayes has been an outspoken supporter for women's rights in sports throughout her career, fighting relentlessly to ensure equal resources, facilities, and respect for women's teams. When she took over at Chelsea, the women's squad had fewer resources than the men's club. She helped Chelsea become one of the most well-supported and financially financed women's teams in England, establishing a precedent for other clubs to follow. Her lobbying has had an impact, persuading clubs throughout the Women's Super League (WSL) to spend more substantially in women's soccer and treat female teams with the same respect as male ones.

Her activism extends to her involvement with the USWNT, where she has joined continuing efforts to ensure equal compensation and respect for female athletes. Hayes views herself not just as a coach but also as a leader in the struggle for gender equality in athletics. "We have a duty to make sure the next generation of girls doesn't face the same limitations we did," she told me. This dedication has solidified her image as a trailblazer, respected not just for her coaching accomplishments but also for her impact on the greater culture of women's sports.

One of Hayes' distinguishing features is her focus on ethics. She has often emphasized the value of justice, decency, and treating others with respect. Her straightforward yet empathetic style has drawn comparisons to renowned managers such as Sir Alex Ferguson, with whom she shares a dedication to fostering a team culture that prioritizes transparency and responsibility. "No one wants to work for a [expletive], it's true," Hayes said amusingly. "We have a choice." Nothing makes me prouder than witnessing these ladies emerge as leaders both on and off the field."

Hayes' legacy as a leader is defined not just by the titles she has earned but also by the people she has affected. She sees her work as a coach as a chance to promote both athletic success and personal development. Her teammates, whether at Chelsea or with the USWNT, have regularly hailed her as a mentor whose advice has stretched beyond soccer, guiding them through their professions and personal lives with strength and honesty.

Chapter 7

Challenges and Overcoming Adversity

Emma Hayes' road to becoming one of the most renowned leaders in women's soccer has been fraught with personal and professional obstacles. Each challenge, from her early days of restricted chances to failures in her coaching career, has honed her resilience, sharpened her sense of purpose, and reaffirmed the principles that characterize her today. Through these experiences, Hayes created a leadership style based on empathy, responsibility, and a relentless pursuit of greatness. Here are some of the important setbacks and obstacles she encountered, as well as the lessons she learned about persistence and resilience along the road.

Emma Hayes started playing soccer when there weren't many possibilities for women in the sport. Growing up in England during the 1980s, she had few role models and little access to professional training. Her passion for soccer set her apart, but she quickly realized that achieving her goals in a sector dominated by men would be challenging. Hayes faced cultural and institutional challenges from the outset, since there were no established avenues for women to seek professional coaching careers. She has commented on this period, stating that she had no female soccer role models other than her mother and that her primary source of motivation in the sport was male players such as Glenn Hoddle.

Despite these obstacles, Hayes remained resolute. She worked relentlessly to improve her talents, finally deciding to continue her soccer career by migrating to the United States and coaching in women's soccer leagues and collegiate teams. Her early experiences taught her the value of tenacity and adaptation. Rather than yielding to the constraints imposed by her surroundings, Hayes forged her own path, a philosophy that would continue to characterize her career.

When Hayes took on her first big head coaching position with the Chicago Red Stars in the Women's Professional Soccer (WPS) league, she encountered significant financing and league stability issues. The WPS faced financial difficulties, and Hayes frequently had to manage with limited resources, balancing the demands of building a robust squad against an uncertain league structure. This experience was challenging as Hayes had to constantly modify her plans and expectations while addressing team management issues that were often beyond her control. Her tenure with the Red Stars came to an end when she left the club, something she had not expected.

When Hayes returned to England to join Chelsea FC Women in 2012, she had another challenge: the women's squad was underfunded, and women's soccer in England was mainly overlooked. The players on her roster often had to work other jobs to support themselves, and resources like training facilities and medical personnel were limited. Hayes saw personally the disparities between men's and women's soccer and became committed to effecting long-term change. Over the years, she battled for improved resources and fair treatment for her squad, establishing a new norm that other teams soon followed.

These events reinforced her conviction in the strength of resilience and the significance of standing up for one's principles, no matter the challenges. Hayes has repeatedly claimed that enduring such difficulties helped her create a distinct sense of purpose—establishing a legacy that assures future generations of female soccer players do not experience the same limits.

One of Hayes' most difficult experiences was during Chelsea FC Women's 2021 season, when the team advanced to the UEFA Women's Champions League final but lost badly to Barcelona. This defeat was a significant blow for Hayes and her squad, who had wanted to win their first Champions League crown. Hayes felt personally accountable for her setback, which made her rethink her methods and decisions. However, she opted to see this event as a lesson in humility and development, one that would benefit both herself and her teammates.

Following the defeat, Hayes instituted a rigorous self-reflection process, requiring herself and her team to critically evaluate what went wrong and how they might better. She pushed her athletes to confront their setbacks with honesty and utilize them as fuel to progress. This process of reflection became a defining event, reinforcing her "no-excuse" culture of responsibility and continual growth. Hayes often stresses that failures are part of the process and that progress comes from facing problems head-on. "Losing is part of winning," she said. "You have to learn how to lose to understand what it takes to win." Personal losses, along with her work successes and setbacks, have challenged Hayes' perseverance. In 2023, her father passed away, leaving her deeply saddened. Hayes, who considers her parents to be important influencers in her life, describes her father as her "biggest supporter" and a constant source of stability throughout her journey. His death came just as she was ready to embark on new career difficulties with the USWNT, and Hayes utilized the incident to draw strength, incorporating her father's memories into her work.

Hayes wore an American eagle necklace at the 2024 Olympics to remember her father, which represented his spirit and wisdom. After guiding the USWNT to a gold medal, she praised her father's memories for providing her the courage to persist throughout the most difficult times. Hayes has expressed how this incident taught her the significance of family and personal perseverance, supporting her view that the people who support and inspire one enhance their purpose.

Key Lessons from Adversity

Hayes' path through personal and professional difficulties has taught her some significant lessons, which she has shared with players, colleagues, and future leaders:

Resilience through Reflection: Hayes believes that progress is achieved by closely examining both accomplishments and setbacks. Hayes founded her "no excuse" culture on the premise that everyone must evaluate their performance and accept responsibility for their actions. This concept, she argues, fosters resilience by enabling individuals to learn from failures without assigning blame.

Hayes' early struggles in women's soccer inspired her to be a strong champion for equality and improved resources for women's teams. Her efforts at Chelsea set a new bar for professionalism in the WSL, pushing other clubs to boost support for their women's teams. Her advocacy highlights that meaningful change often involves perseverance and a willingness to question the status quo.

The Value of Joy and Unity: Hayes has constantly stressed the importance of joy and connection in teams, believing that a positive atmosphere improves both mental health and performance. Her approach with the USWNT, based on "belief, freedom, and fun," helped her players gain confidence and togetherness. This encounter reinforces her notion that resilience is not just about overcoming problems but also about discovering pleasure and strength in the process.

Hayes has found purpose in personal connections, as her losses and trials have taught her the value of family, friends, and mentors. Her father's influence continues to guide her, and she often finds strength in the connections she's formed during her career. Hayes' experience demonstrates how our interactions with others may increase our sense of purpose.

Emma Hayes' tenacity and purpose-driven attitude have characterized her profession while also setting an encouraging example for anybody confronting difficulties. Her journey exemplifies how development necessitates failures, and how contemplation, activism, and supportive connections can uncover meaning.

Chapter 8

Wealth and Financial Legacy

C lever career moves, expanding sponsorship agreements, and setting new coaching salary records have distinguished Emma Hayes' path to financial success. As her coaching career advanced, her financial means grew, allowing her to not only live comfortably but also make substantial contributions to humanitarian organizations that reflected her principles.

Hayes' first fortune stemmed from her time with Chelsea FC Women, when she established herself as one of the world's finest female managers. By 2024, she was earning between £200,000 and £300,000 per year, making her one of the highest-paid coaches in women's soccer. However, her promotion to the United States Women's National Team (USWNT) in 2023 was a significant step forward. Her new post allegedly pays her up to $2 million per year, putting her on pace with U.S. men's national coach Gregg Berhalter, a trailblazer for female pay equity in the profession. This pay shows not just her stature as a talented tactician but also her worth in a competitive coaching market, particularly following her Olympic victories with the USWNT.

In addition to her teaching duties, Hayes has promoted well-known companies such as Nike and Visa, which has contributed to her financial security. Although information about these agreements is sparse, her collaborations with such large businesses demonstrate her importance in women's sports. Before beginning her long-term career with Chelsea, she also held a temporary position at her family's London-based currency exchange firm, Covent Garden FX. Her family's firm gave her both experience and supplemental cash early in her career, allowing her to diversify her finances before returning full-time to coaching.

Hayes has led a very modest life, focusing her money and influence on professional advancement and charity rather than public excess. Her financial success has enabled her to lobby for more resources, better facilities, and fair pay for women's soccer. At Chelsea, she advocated for the women's squad to have similar access to resources, including training and medical facilities, as the men's team. Her efforts helped Chelsea FC Women get more backing, inspiring other teams in the Women's Super League (WSL) to follow suit and prioritize investing in women's soccer.

Hayes has also been involved in philanthropic efforts, concentrating on youth development and pushing for gender equality in sports. Though her public philanthropic actions are less well-documented, her activism for gender equality and fair treatment in soccer is consistent with her social impact principles. She frequently discusses the importance of increasing opportunities for young girls in sports, and she actively participates in programs that promote fair access to soccer resources for women and girls worldwide. Hayes utilizes her position and financial success to advocate for equitable pay and opportunity, therefore encouraging structural improvements that benefit women's sports in general.

In essence, Emma Hay's financial career demonstrates a dedication to her ideals. Her income and assets provide her with not just personal security but also the capacity to have a positive social influence inside and outside of the soccer community. Throughout her career, Hayes has demonstrated how she can use her financial success to advocate for change, promote equality, and leave a legacy that benefits future generations.

Chapter 9

Enduring Legacy and Impact

E mma Hayes has made a lasting imprint on soccer, transforming not just her teams but the whole landscape of women's sports with her ideas and leadership. Beyond the field, people recognize her not only for her tactical skill but also for the long-term impact of her values—resilience, discipline, joy, and a dedication to equality.

Hayes' journey began in England, where she encountered a society that offered limited opportunities for women in soccer. Overcoming these obstacles, she went on to head Chelsea FC Women for nearly a decade, building the club into a dominating force that won six Women's Super League (WSL) crowns, five FA Cups, and played at the highest European levels. Her efforts at Chelsea boosted the club and redefined what a women's squad was capable of, setting new standards for female athlete training, facilities, and support. By fighting for these improvements, she helped to alter perceptions and urge other clubs to invest more seriously in women's teams, setting a precedent for the league and encouraging other organizations to treat women's soccer with equal attention and resources.

Hayes took over as head coach of the United States Women's National Team (USWNT) in 2024, and he led the team to Olympic gold. Her athletes credit their success to her inspiring concept of "belief, freedom, and fun." Hayes' attitude enabled each player to express himself and execute with confidence, reviving a squad that had previously struggled. Her influence on the USWNT has led to a cultural transformation, with players praising her presence for revitalizing team chemistry and bringing out their best qualities. Young players on the United States under-20 team also highlight her Olympic achievements as an influence, exposing how her beliefs and work ethic inspire the next generation of players to strive for greatness with "heart, determination, and grit."

Colleagues and fans often compare Hayes to iconic individuals such as Sir Alex Ferguson, whose long-term success at Manchester United mirrors her approach at Chelsea. Similar to Ferguson, Hayes' strong yet caring management approach fosters responsibility and trust. Her "no excuse" culture, a defining feature of her ideology, pushes players to self-reflect and continually develop without assigning blame. This culture of reflection and accountability has struck a deep chord with her players, distinguishing her as a leader who seeks to build well-rounded persons rather than just winning. This notion of self-accountability has had a long-lasting impact, motivating athletes and coaches outside her own teams to uphold similar standards in their own professions and lives.

Her impact extends to promoting gender equality in sports. Hayes has accelerated the transition to more equal treatment of female athletes by fighting for fair pay, resources, and respect. Her leadership in this area is part of a broader legacy that has inspired not just her players but also other coaches and organizations. Her former coworkers, players, and even competition see her as a pioneer who helped open doors and establish a professional atmosphere in which women's soccer could flourish. This legacy of activism and equality continues to inspire future players, who view Hayes as evidence that determination can influence the system in positive ways.

Hayes' colleagues and teammates express respect and thanks for her achievements. USWNT players Trinity Rodman and Mallory Swanson have characterized her effect as transformational, stating that her combination of professionalism, fun, and discipline produced a team atmosphere that felt like family. Hayes' players value her not just as a coach but also as a mentor whose advice helps them improve both on and off the court. This statement echoes throughout her tenure at Chelsea and the USWNT, underscoring the

31

significant personal impact she has had on countless lives.

Her ability to inspire, her tireless pursuit of greatness, and her unwavering commitment to equality form the foundation of Emma Hayes' legacy. Through her work, she has demonstrated that success is not solely based on competence, but also on integrity, resilience, and a lifelong commitment to empowering others. Her legacy will endure, motivating future generations to approach their occupations with purpose, compassion, and a desire to help people around them.

Chapter 10

Behind the Scenes: Lesser-Known Stories

E mma Hayes is well-known for her intense competition, leadership abilities, and commitment to sports equality, but a few lesser-known areas of her life illustrate the complexity of her personality and distinct teaching style. Here are some unexpected and intimate details about her life, interests, and personal peculiarities that give depth to her already outstanding legacy.

Despite being most known for her soccer achievements, Hayes is a lifelong learner with interests that extend beyond sports. For example, when coaching at Iona College, she constantly pursued opportunities to improve her communication and leadership abilities. She is known for consistently developing her talents and incorporating lessons from a variety of sectors, including psychology, management, and even personal relationships, into her coaching approach. These influences are evident in her ability to foster a close-knit team atmosphere in which players feel appreciated and understood, while combining technical skill with emotional intelligence in her interactions with players and staff.

Despite her serious public appearance, Hayes' colleagues and players say she has a fantastic sense of humor. This aspect of her personality is important in developing camaraderie among her teams. She routinely employs comedy to break the ice and keep spirits up, especially in high-pressure circumstances. Hayes, known for her jokes and laid-back manner during training sessions, has gained a reputation for playfully referring to herself as a "modern-day Sir Alex Ferguson" and comparing her managing career and commitment to Ferguson's stint at Manchester United. Both managers, Hayes and Ferguson, have a steadfast dedication to their teams, balancing discipline with personal concern for their players' well-being.

Hayes' "no-excuse" attitude, which she developed at Chelsea and now with the U.S. Women's National Team, displays her strong conviction in individual responsibility. Hayes often used metaphors such as "holding up a mirror" after each game to persuade her players to reflect on their conduct rather than assign blame. Her own experience, where she consistently held herself accountable for her actions and responded to setbacks without becoming frustrated, inspired this approach. Her players often identify this approach as a fundamental reason for their respect for her and their own personal development, praising Hayes as a leader who holds high standards while providing a secure place for them to thrive.

Hayes' family is crucial to her life, and her relationship with them remains a guiding influence, notably her involvement in her family's company, a currency exchange operation in London. Though soccer became her primary focus, Hayes briefly worked in the family company, where she gained valuable business skills and established a feeling of responsibility that she carried over into her coaching career. This connection to her origins and community remains strong; she credits her family with instilling in her the qualities of loyalty, resilience, and a no-nonsense work ethic.

Hayes has also been an outspoken champion for women's representation outside of athletics, particularly in technology. She often talks at events focusing on female leadership and empowerment, emphasizing the significance of diversity in all sectors, particularly in historically male-dominated professions such as technology. Her advocacy work has motivated young women to seek careers in sports and technology, and her lectures often rely on her personal experiences in breaking down obstacles and establishing credibility in a competitive sector.

When not on the field, Hayes enjoys cooking and regularly experiments with various dishes as a method of relaxation. Her love of cooking reflects her concept of making time for personal development and balance, which is essential in her high-stakes work. She also dedicates herself to maintaining her physical fitness, engaging in daily jogging and yoga sessions. These interests, she claims, offer mental clarity and help her cope with the physical and emotional demands of her job, enabling her to give her all to her colleagues and family.

Hayes' focus on pleasure distinguishes her approach to soccer. While many coaches emphasize discipline and energy, Hayes feels that success stems from players who really like the game. This attitude contributed significantly to the success of the US Women's National Team under her direction. Hayes urges her players to be comfortable during training and pre-game practices, often playing music while they warm up and sometimes joining in to create a positive atmosphere. This playful attitude, which is unique at the top level, demonstrates her awareness of the psychological components of performance. It's a strategy her players value and credit with increasing their confidence and team spirit.

One of the most touching anecdotes from Hayes' life is her concern for her teammates' well-being. When former Chelsea player Katie Chapman struggled to balance her professional career and family life, Hayes pushed for her, urging the club to provide support and flexibility so Chapman could continue to play. This example exemplifies Hayes' dedication not just to her players' athletic success but also to their personal lives and happiness, demonstrating that her approach is both compassionate and effective. These stories underscore Hayes' holistic coaching philosophy, which determines success not by trophies but by the long-term positive impact on her players' lives.

Emma Hayes' reputation extends beyond her tactical genius. She is redefining success in athletics by infusing values such as joy, resilience, and personal development into her coaching. Her effort has inspired not just her teammates but also a worldwide audience of fans, coaches, and young athletes who see her as a role model for both her talents and her humanity. From her amusing quips to her unwavering dedication to responsibility, Hayes' life exemplifies the concept that success in sports—and in life—comes not just from winning but also from motivating people around you to fulfill their greatest potential.

In conclusion, these private and lesser-known aspects of Emma Hayes' life enrich her tale, making her an inspirational figure for aspiring athletes, coaches, and fans alike. Her distinct personality and ideals continue to reverberate well beyond the pitch, leaving a legacy that promotes both achievement and empathy in equal measure.

Chapter 11

Frequently Asked Questions (FAQ)

1. Was Emma Hayes a professional soccer player before becoming a coach?

At seventeen, a ski accident cut short Hayes' soccer career, leaving him with an ankle injury. This early failure prompted her to change her career path and focus on teaching rather than playing professionally.

2. Is her achievement entirely due to Chelsea's funding?

Although Chelsea's investment was beneficial, Hayes had to battle for resources for the women's squad. Her strategic vision and determination in assembling a competitive team enabled her success, not simply the finances.

3. Did she always want to be a coach?

Coaching was not her first choice. Initially, she wanted to play professionally, but an accident interrupted her plans, allowing her to discover her ability and love for teaching while in college.

4. Is she as harsh and tough as she appears?

Known for her "no excuse" culture, Hayes also fosters enjoyment and well-being. She often adds comedy and music into training, striking a balance between discipline and delight to build a healthy team dynamic.

5. How does she compare to Sir Alex Ferguson?

Indeed, Hayes' long-term vision, perseverance, and ability to foster a cohesive team environment often draw comparisons to Ferguson. Like Ferguson, she established discipline and responsibility in her squad, leaving an indelible mark at Chelsea.

6. Does she have a personal life other than soccer?

Yes, Hayes values family time with her husband and likes hobbies such as cooking and walking, which she says help her cope with the high expectations of her job.

7. Does she participate in youth development?

Hayes has traditionally promoted young development, fostering players like Fran Kirby and Bethany England. She feels that early assistance for young players is critical to their development into top-level athletes.

8. Does she push for gender equality?

Absolutely. Hayes has been a prominent champion for equal pay, resources, and respect in women's soccer, both at Chelsea and with the USWNT, working to raise the sport's standards.

9. What influence did she have on the USWNT?

Her presence with the USWNT energized the squad by emphasizing "belief, freedom, and fun." Players thank her for bringing them together and inspiring them, resulting in their 2024 Olympic gold medal.

10. Is her coaching philosophy based only on tactics?

Hayes combines tactical competence and emotional insight. She focuses on the mental and emotional components of the game, teaching players resilience, pleasure, and self-confidence.

11. How does she manage loss?

Hayes turns setbacks into learning opportunities, enabling her athletes to self-reflect and concentrate on ongoing progress. This developing attitude is an essential component of her worldview.

12. Did she exclusively play for Chelsea before joining the USWNT?

No, Hayes previously coached the Long Island Lady Riders, Iona College, and the Chicago Red Stars before joining Chelsea in 2012.

13. Has she recently found success in coaching?

Hayes has had years of success as Chelsea dominates the WSL and foreign tournaments. Her latest triumphs with the USWNT add to a lengthy list of accomplishments.

14. Does she believe mental health is crucial in sports?

Yes, Hayes promotes mental health, encouraging her players to find pleasure in soccer and assisting them in juggling personal and athletic responsibilities.

15. What is her soccer legacy?

Hayes' legacy is multidimensional, including tactical genius, activism for gender equality, and her impact on the culture of female athletics. We expect her influence to inspire future generations of athletes and coaches globally.

APPENDICES

1. Chronology of Key Life Events

- 1976: Born in Camden, London, England.
- 1997-2001: Began her coaching journey with Liverpool Hope University's women's team while studying, followed by youth development roles at Corydon and Crystal Palace.
- 2001-2003: First professional coaching position with the Long Island Lady Riders in the U.S.
- 2008: Appointed head coach for the Chicago Red Stars in the Women's Professional Soccer (WPS) league.
- 2012: Became the manager of Chelsea FC Women, marking the start of a transformative period for the team.
- 2015: Chelsea FC Women secured their first FA Cup and WSL title, establishing Hayes as a trailblazing coach.
- 2021: Guided Chelsea to their first-ever UEFA Women's Champions League final and was named the Best FIFA Women's Coach.
- 2023: Transitioned from Chelsea to become the head coach of the U.S. Women's National Team (USWNT).
- 2024: Led the USWNT to a gold medal at the Paris Olympics, marking her most significant career accomplishment. Hayes also received the inaugural Women's Ballon d'Or for Coach of the Year.

2. Major Awards and Honors

- Women's Ballon d'Or Coach of the Year (2024): First recipient of this award, celebrating her contributions to both Chelsea and the USWNT.
- FIFA Best Women's Coach (2021): Recognized for her exceptional leadership and success with Chelsea.
- Order of the British Empire (OBE): Received in 2022 for her contributions to women's soccer and advocacy for gender equality, having previously been awarded an MBE in 2016.
- FA WSL Manager of the Season: Multiple-time recipient, including for Chelsea's undefeated domestic campaigns.
- FA WSL Hall of Fame Inductee (2021): Honored for her lasting impact on the league and her achievements in women's soccer.

3. Key publications and media contributions

Emma Hayes is a respected voice in soccer commentary, having appeared as a pundit for major tournaments like Euro 2020. Her insights on tactical strategies and leadership have broadened her influence, making her a prominent figure in soccer analysis.

4. List of Notable Team Players under Hayes

Throughout her Chelsea tenure and USWNT role, Hayes has coached and mentored numerous high-profile players, including:

- Fran Kirby: English forward nurtured by Hayes into an internationally recognized player.
- Sam Kerr: Australian star and key player in Chelsea's WSL success.
- Bethany England: English forward, whom Hayes supported from youth to professional levels.
- Sophia Smith, Lindsey Horan, and Mallory Swanson: Key players for the USWNT who thrived under Hayes' leadership.

5. Index of Significant People and Places

- Liverpool Hope University: Where Hayes began her career and realized her potential as a coach.
- Bruce Buck: Former Chelsea FC chairman who supported Hayes in transforming the Chelsea Women's team.
- USWNT: A major chapter in her career, where she led the team to an Olympic gold medal and reestablished them as a top international team's.

6. Family Tree and Personal Connections

Emma Hayes maintains a strong family connection. Her husband is a private yet integral supporter of her career. She has a son, born in 2016, who adds balance to her life amidst the demands of coaching. Hayes also credits her late father for her resilience, dedicating her 2024 Olympic victory to his memory.

7. Recent Awards, Nominations, and Achievements (2024)

- Women's Ballon d'Or Coach of the Year: Awarded for her successes with Chelsea and the USWNT.
- Olympic Gold Medal (Paris 2024): Led the USWNT to victory, a career-defining moment that she described as "bigger than anything else I have ever done."
- Top FIFA Ranking for USWNT: Under Hayes, the USWNT reclaimed the No. 1 spot in the FIFA rankings, showcasing her immediate positive impact on the team.

8. Reference Section for Further Exploration

For a more detailed look into Emma Hayes' life and career, consider the following resources:

- FIFA and Chelsea FC official sites for her biography, achievements, and recent awards.

- BBC Sports, Sky Sports, and NBC Olympics for in-depth articles on her coaching philosophy and legacy.
- SBI Soccer and 101 Great Goals for coverage on her Olympic gold with the USWNT and recent achievements.

BIBLIOGRAPHY

1. Books and publications.

- "A Completely Different Game: My Leadership Playbook" Written by Emma Hayes, this book explores her unique approach to leadership, blending her personal journey with insights on managing high-performance teams, overcoming challenges, and advocating for women in sports. It's both a leadership guide and a personal memoir, reflecting Hayes' journey from Chelsea to the U.S. Women's National Team (USWNT) (Amazon, 2024).
- "Kill the Unicorn": This book, available on Goodreads, further delves into Hayes' views on collaborative success over individual heroism, arguing for teamwork as the core of lasting achievements. Hayes offers a detailed perspective on managing elite athletes, highlighting challenges and unique issues in women's sports.

2. Documentaries and video series

- "The Blueprint" is a Chelsea FC-produced three-part documentary that chronicles Hayes' transformative 10-year journey with Chelsea FC women. This behind-the-scenes series includes interviews with Hayes and key players, giving viewers an inside look at her leadership style and the challenges faced in elevating Chelsea to elite status. Available on

44

Chelsea FC's website.

- U.S. Women's National Team Profiles: Coverage from the 2024 Paris Olympics features Hayes' reflections and strategic insights as she led the team to victory. Interviews and match breakdowns highlight her coaching impact and the cultural shift she introduced to the team, showcasing her philosophy in action (NBC Olympics).

3. Articles and interviews.

- "How to Be a Good Leader: According to USWNT Coach Emma Hayes" Published by Fast Company, this article outlines Hayes' values in leadership with practical advice that extends beyond sports to any team-focused environment.
- "The Unseen Emma Hayes"—The T Telegraph offers a candid look at Hayes' personality, covering her experiences with adversity, her commitment to mental health, and her advocacy for gender equality in sports.

4. Related biographies and documentaries.

- "What It Takes: The Inspiring Journey of Sarina Wiegman and the Lionesses' Rise to Success" Though not focused on Hayes, this biography explores the journey of another influential female coach in women's soccer. It's a useful complementary read for understanding the challenges faced by women in sports leadership.
- "Everything Your Coach Never Told You Because You're a Girl" by Dan Blank A guide for young female athletes, this book resonates with Hayes' ethos of resilience, empowerment, and building a legacy in sports.

5. Charitable organizations and social causes.

- Women in Sport is a UK-based charity that promotes equality in sports by supporting female athletes and advocating for fair representation. Hayes has frequently collaborated with such organizations, working to uplift the next generation of female athletes.
- Chelsea Foundation: This foundation is dedicated to using soccer to engage and inspire communities through education, health, and inclusion programs. As a former Chelsea coach, Hayes supported their initiatives, which align with her advocacy for sports as a vehicle for social change.

Made in the USA
Middletown, DE
02 December 2024

65813770R00031